Bravo! At last, a great book on a subject that affects everyone in this fast-paced modern world. Most of us are not aware of the need to manage our stress-filled lives until it becomes a problem.

As an air traffic controller for over 25 years, I have seen the effects of stress, personally, and on my colleagues. Having been involved in the Critical Incident Stress Management Team at our workplace, I have seen, very graphically, the different outcomes for individuals who are exposed to stress. The people who have effectively managed their stress continue to thrive in a demanding and stressful occupation. Those who have not managed their stress, have made an early departure from the workplace, with far-reaching implications for the quality of their personal lives.

Before you can effectively manage stress, you must first understand what it is and how it affects you. Only then can you embark on effective stress management.

Martin's book provides simple solutions to leading a full and productive life unaffected by the silent crippler: STRESS.

—Gordon Hay, Air Traffic Controller

Recognizing & Managing Your Stress

"What Do You Mean, I'm Stressed?"

Martin Lesperance

Safety Health Publishing Inc.

Recognizing & Managing Your Stress

"What Do You Mean, I'm Stressed?"

Martin Lesperance

Safety Health Publishing Inc.

Published by: Safety Health Publishing Inc.
Calgary, Alberta. 1-888-278-8964

Canadian Cataloguing in Publication Data

Lesperance, Martin, 1953-

Includes index.
ISBN 0-9698989-2-4

1. Stress management. 2. Stress (Psychology) I. Title.
RA785.L47 1999   155.9'042   C99-910108-0

Editor: Anita Jenkins
Design, layout, production editing: Heather Markham
Illustrations: Jacqueline Dube
Printing: Hignell Printing, Winnipeg

DISCLAIMER
The author and publisher have checked with sources believed to be reliable in a conscientious effort to provide information that is complete and congruent with acceptable standards at the time of publication. However, the dynamic nature of this information leads us to anticipate future changes and updates. Therefore, readers are encouraged to confer with other reliable sources to ensure that they will receive complete, accurate and current information.

Acknowledgements

The following are people I would like to thank for their help with this book. Dr. David Hall, of the Cochrane Learning Centre, for his ideas and for reviewing the material. Dr. June Donaldson, for her suggestions and input. Gordon Hay, air traffic controller, who for 25 years has made me feel safe when I fly. Dayle Hawkins, for pointing out the obvious when it was in front of my nose. Debbie Debnam at Global Training Centre, if I could manage stress like you, Debbie, I'd be a lot better off. To Valerie Cade Lee, for her encouragement. To Anita Jenkins for the editing, Heather Markham for the layout and design, and Jacqueline Dube for the illustrations.

Table of Contents

Foreword

My personal involvement with this book increased enormously between the time Martin Lesperance first asked me to design and produce it and the time when it was published.

In the spring of 1998, Martin and I met and agreed on the initial design concepts. Shortly after that, my husband, at 46 years young, had severe angina. The next few months brought quadruple bypass surgery and a major change in our family's lifestyle. Like most people who suffer a cardiac event, we had been totally unprepared.

Of the seven risk factors, he had only three. This led us to believe that stress was likely a major factor.

After the crisis was over and I was ready to continue working on Martin's book, I read it again—from a completely different perspective. Now, I had seen the effects of stress in my own household.

You're not too young (and it's never too late) to start looking at how stress can affect your life.

—Heather Markham

Introduction

People have always had to deal with stress. Cave men were worried that a big, fuzzy bear might walk into the cave in the middle of the night. People living in the middle ages had a big concern about contracting the plague. And early settlers were stressed about surviving the harsh winter or anything else that Mother Nature might throw at them.

But stress is now being discussed more than ever before. Today, stress is not usually about surviving the winter or outrunning a bear. Instead, it involves problems in the family or at work, financial or health problems, and much more.

When Beaver Cleaver was a boy, life seemed easy. In the *Leave it to Beaver* TV series, once you got a job, there was a good chance you would have that job for life, and a good pension to boot. In most families, only one parent had to work to provide a comfortable living. You didn't have to worry about owning two cars because no one else did. It seems it was easier to keep up with the Cleavers than with the current neighbors, the Joneses.

Now, most families cannot survive on one income. Both parents have to work. The high divorce rate has produced more one-parent families, where the main caregiver may have a reduced income and bigger responsibilities. The single parent has to find a good daycare, wonder if there is enough time to meet with the teacher when a child is having problems in school and handle hundreds of other such details, often without the help of the other parent.

Some people come close to bragging about how busy they are and how little sleep they are getting. Companies are reducing their payrolls and asking workers to do more with less. There are no free rides in the workplace.

As Bob Dylan said in the 1960s, "The times they are a changin'." There isn't much chance that things will change back to what they were during the Cleavers' generation. We have to deal with the present. One of the first steps is to recognize that things have changed and accept the changes instead of fighting them.

Many physicians estimate that up to 75% of patient visits can be traced back to stress-related problems. Companies are paying millions of dollars to people who miss work because of stress. Most importantly, stress can ruin families and cause pain and suffering for people who are close to the person who is under stress.

Stress can be contagious. If you are living with a stressed person, your stress level may also increase.

■ ■ ■

"Try as you will, you get behind in the race, in spite of yourself. It's an incessant strain to keep pace...And you still lose ground. Science empties its discoveries on you so fast that you stagger beneath them in hopeless bewilderment...Everything is high pressure. Human nature can't endure much more. —Atlantic Journal, June 16, 1833

2

What is stress?

DEFINITION

Richard Lazarus of the University of California defines stress as "a state we experience when the demands that are made upon us cannot be counterbalanced by our ability to deal with them" (as quoted in *I'm Too Busy to Be Stressed* by Dr. Hillary Jones).

The demands we perceive may be real or imaginary. In either case, it is how we respond to the demands that determines whether stress will get the better of us. Some people thrive on the stress of a nearing project deadline. Others who are facing the same demands will lose sleep, have a decreased appetite, and go home and kick the dog. We are all different. Different things push our buttons.

SHORT-TERM AND LONG-TERM STRESS

Everyone has stress in their lives. The only people who feel no stress whatsoever are dead and happily buried or in a coma. Some stress is very short term. For example:

- While trying to make an important phone call, you constantly receive a busy signal.
- You are walking down a dark alley. Three rough-looking hoodlums who are following you mention that they would like to see your wallet.
- You are in a traffic jam and late for an appointment.

- Your boss dumps an unexpected project on you. (If the project is big, this could become long-term stress.)

Other stress can be long term, as in these examples:

- There are threats of layoffs at work.
- You have made a career change within your organization.
- You are unhappy with your child care situation.
- Your elderly mother has just moved in with you.
- You constantly face serious money problems.
- You are looking after a seriously ill or injured family member.
- You are seriously injured or ill.
- Your spouse wants a divorce and you don't.
- You hate your job and/or your boss.

GOOD STRESS (EUSTRESS)

Not all stress is bad. You need some stress in your life to keep you healthy and feeling alive. You need a reason to get out of bed in the morning. This is an example of good stress:

You're at the top of a very steep ski run. You notice your heart pumping, and your senses are keen. Your body is ready for the run. You make the run, test your limits and feel great. You feel excited and alive.

Working on a project that is going well can produce good stress. You feel confident in your abilities, and that everything is under control. But if the project runs into major problems as the deadline approaches, what was once good stress may turn into bad stress. You now feel a loss of control.

BAD STRESS (DISTRESS)

Bad stress develops when you feel you can't control the situation. For example, you may feel overwhelmed in the face of an impending layoff. You become angry, worried or tense. You find that you are thinking about the situation all the time. When your mind is in this state, it affects your body. Physical problems develop. Unless you can recognize bad stress and learn to manage it, big trouble awaits you. Be aware of the pressures you put on yourself.

WHO IS PRONE TO STRESS?

Some people are more prone to stress than others. One attempt to explain this is the Type A and Type B personality studies done in the U.S. in the 1950s. When American cardiologists Mayer Friedman and Ray Rosenman collected information about 1500 men, they found that their subjects fell into two groups with distinctively different traits. The "Type A" personalities seemed more prone to heart attacks.

Type A personalities:

- are hard-driving
- want to achieve as many things as possible (high achievers)
- tend to become irritated and angry over seemingly minor things
- tend to put personal goals and careers before family and friends
- become impatient when listening to others
- are not observant about little things
- are perfectionists
- like to be busy; have a hard time relaxing
- do several things at once (e.g., eating while working)
- are critical of other people and of themselves
- are impatient
- are very competitive (e.g., playing games to win)

In their excellent book *Anger Kills*, Drs. Redford and Virginia Williams say the "hostility" trait in Type A personalities is especially dangerous, as it seems to increase the risk of cardiovascular disease.

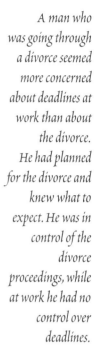

A man who was going through a divorce seemed more concerned about deadlines at work than about the divorce. He had planned for the divorce and knew what to expect. He was in control of the divorce proceedings, while at work he had no control over deadlines.

Type B personalities:

- are laid back and bothered by very few things (In a traffic jam, a Type B person might just say, "Oh, well.")
- are usually happy with less
- are not as competitive and play for fun, not caring if they lose the game
- can relax without feeling guilty
- do not feel a sense of urgency or that they just don't have enough time

Clearly, Type B personalities tend to be more relaxed than Type A people. There is some of both Types A and B in most people, but one type will be more dominant.

WHAT STRESSES YOU; WHAT STRESSES ME

"We all boil at different temperatures."
—Ralph Waldo Emerson

Numerous things can increase a person's stress level: different things bother different people. Let's take a look at some of the more common events that increase stress. I'm sure you will be able to add to the list.

Family stress

Although family is a major source of strength for most people, it is also the source of much of our stress.

Divorce. Almost half of all marriages end in divorce, and few events in life are more stressful, especially if the divorce is messy. Every aspect of the lives of the people involved will be changed.

Bad relationships. Not all bad marriages end in divorce. For different reasons, people decide to stay married even though the bad times are outnumbering the good. In these types of relationships, just the sight of your spouse may be enough to get you wound up. And even if you are in a good relationship, little things can cause stress.

Birth of a child. Anyone who has raised children will agree that the birth of a child certainly changes the way things are done in a household. Parents of a young child get less sleep, for example, and that increases stress levels.

Teenagers know everything there is to know and their parents know nothing. Their wish to flex their independence muscles increases the stress level in many homes.

Parents. Aging parents often end up living with their children. No matter how much love there is between parents and their children, this can be quite a difficult time for all involved.

In-laws. More than a few people have trouble with their in-laws. This can be an ongoing problem leading to frequent arguments between spouses.

Financial stress

Many families living close to the poverty line are under constant stress because of a lack of money. However, people who make a very good living may also have serious money problems. People seem to want more and more. The more money they make, the more they spend—on bigger and nicer homes, newer cars, more expensive holidays, expensive jewelry and other things that not do not necessarily make them happier.

In many cases, financial stress is easy to manage. Simply live within your means. Do you really need the $20,000 power boat that you use twelve times a year? Could you manage to survive in a house that costs $30,000 less? Do you really need that trip to Hawaii this year? Yes, these things are nice to have, but if they significantly increase your stress, are they really worth it?

You might consider consulting a financial advisor about planning a budget and getting your financial situation under control.

"I once complained because I had no shoes, until I met a man who had no feet."
—Author unknown

"Never keep up with the Joneses. Drag them down to your level. It's cheaper."
—Quentin Crisp

Physical stress. A person doesn't need to have a physically hard job to become physically stressed. Many people who work 60 hours a week at a desk job become physically stressed, especially if they are not getting enough sleep, have a poor diet or are not getting enough exercise.

Keeping in shape gives you the extra energy you need to get you through stressful times. When you're in shape, you feel better about yourself. If you don't already participate in an exercise program, plan now to do so.

THIS FEELS GREAT!

Death. Nothing rates higher on the stress scale than the death of your spouse or child. This is an incredibly hard time for people. The death of a close friend can also be devastating.

Job stress and job changes. As a result of the downsizing trend in many companies, thousands of people have been laid off and the remaining workers are expected to do more with less. Workplaces have changed. People who stick with the old saying, "I don't like change," are finding themselves out of a job.

Environmental stress. Living in a neighborhood that has a high crime rate. Working in a small, cramped and noisy office. Having your spouse's friends and their five children come to visit for a month ... Your environment can definitely add to your stress.

A man shot himself in the head and died. Later, it was learned that the man had lost his job and then his wife left him, taking the kids. The stress of these two major events added up to more than he could handle by himself.

Cumulative effects of stress. Many people have to deal with more than one type of stress. Stress has a way of accumulating: one form of stress seems to come along just when you are already struggling with another.

Several stressors, large or small, when left unchecked, can add up to big-time trouble. Before you know it, you're ready to blow. It's important to deal with challenges when they come up. Don't wait. They won't go away by themselves.

Warning! If at any time you feel just too overwhelmed, that life is not worth living or that you might harm yourself, seek professional help immediately.

THE WORKING WOMAN AND STRESS

In the many families where both parents work, there is extra stress, especially for women. A common concern is the care of children. Starting work at 7:00 a.m. and working until 6:00 p.m. is hard enough. Add to that dropping the children off at daycare and picking them up after work. Then take them home and play with them before giving them a bath and putting them to bed. Then, there are just two more loads of laundry before you finish your report for an important client. At last, it's bed time.

In bed, your husband leans over and tells you what a busy day he had. He barely made it to the golf course on time. You consider killing him but you don't like the idea of prison.

The alarm goes off at 5:00 a.m., and it starts all over again.

Who wouldn't be stressed in a situation like this?

In two-career households, communication is crucial. Ground rules have to be set and followed. The work load has to be divided up. Let your spouse know how you feel. Don't wait until it is too late. The earlier you discuss problems, the better off you will be.

I have to constantly juggle being a writer with being a wife and mother. It's a matter of putting two different things first, simultaneously.
—Madeleine L'Engle

> *"I know God will not give me anything I can't handle. I just wish that he didn't trust me so much."*
> *—Mother Theresa*

3

The Cost
of Stress

A man who was working on his doctoral thesis had been under intense stress for a month. He was trying to cope with exams, financial problems, deadlines and more. As he worked, he could hear his infant son crying. The constant crying upset the man more and more. Nothing would soothe the baby. Finally, in frustration, the man grabbed the infant and shook him violently until he stopped crying. The baby later died of brain damage (Shaken Baby Syndrome). In this case, the man's stress cost him his child's life.

Although this is an extreme example, many incidents of violence occur when people are under stress. It costs our society billions of dollars to deal with substance abuse, divorce, motor vehicle collisions, incidents of violence, injuries and frequent visits to the doctor—all problems that may be attributed to stress.

Stress among workers results in alcoholism, absenteeism, lateness, employee turnover, lowered morale, disabilities and even premature death. All of these problems can cost companies millions of dollars, and in the long term these costs affect every employee.

Edward A. Charlesworth and Ronald G. Nathan (*Stress Management*) report that American industry suffers the following losses each year:

- $19.4 billion because of premature death
- $15.6 billion because of alcoholism
- $15 billion because of stress-related absenteeism

Also, millions of dollars are spent each year to recruit replacements for executives who have heart disease. In Canada, workers miss an average of five days' work per year due to stress and personal problems.

These figures are staggering. And, in addition to the loss of dollars, stress often results in immeasurable human suffering. As a paramedic, I have been called to domestic disputes that were extremely disturbing. Horrible things can happen to families that are under stress. Imagine what harm is done to children whose parents hurt them because of stress that they failed to manage.

THE FIGHT OR FLIGHT SYNDROME

Cave men and cave women had a lot to be stressed about. They had to worry about their fire going out, keeping warm and getting enough to eat. They also had to worry about being eaten by saber-toothed tigers. Back then, if a cave bear was chasing you, you had to have one of two very important qualities. You had to be very good a fighter and know how to swing a big club with dazzling speed and bite as hard as Mike Tyson. Or, you had to be a very fast runner, without the help of steroids.

Because some people had neither of these qualities, the human body had to compensate. It developed something known as the Fight or Flight syndrome. When times get hectic or you are excited, your sympathetic nervous system and adrenalin kick into high gear. This response gave the cave man the extra boost of energy he needed to fight the bear or run away from him, or deal with any other kind of trouble that came along.

There aren't many saber-toothed tigers now, but there are other things that can worry us. Have you ever:

■ Been followed by a gang of rough-looking youths on a dark, deserted street?

■ Lost control of your car on an icy road and narrowly avoided a head-on collision with a semi-trailer?

■ Been scared to death about giving a speech?

■ Had to fire an employee?

■ Been fired?

DID YOU SAY... MOVE!?

In situations like these, you have probably noticed your heart pounding and your breathing speeding up. This happens because your sympathetic nervous system (Fight or Flight syndrome) has kicked in.

Whether the threat is real or imagined, adrenalin is released into the blood stream from the adrenal glands (small glands above your kidneys). Adrenalin does amazing things to your body:

- Your **heart** beats faster and harder, and your pulse races. More blood is pumped to your muscles so you can run faster. This is why adrenalin is used as a stimulant for people in cardiac arrest. (When used for this purpose it is often called epinephrine.)

- The increased pumping of the heart raises your **blood pressure**.

- Your **breathing** speeds up and gets deeper so you can suck in more air, just in case your muscles are planning to do some extra work such as running for your life. The adrenalin also dilates or widens your air passages to allow you to breathe more air into your lungs. (Adrenalin is used for people who are allergic to foods, bee stings and other substances because it helps to dilate the air passages that swell up in a severe allergic reaction.)

- Because it takes a lot of energy and blood flow to digest, you may feel tired after eating a big meal. When you are scared or nervous, the last thing you think about is food. Your **digestive system** shuts down, so the blood can go to the large muscles. Since one of the first stages of digestion is saliva production, you may have a dry mouth. Many public speakers keep a glass of water close by for this reason.

- In anticipation of the extra work you may have to do in a threatening situation, your body deals with potential heat build-up by **sweating**. Consequently, you may sweat when you are nervous. Even though you are not doing any physical work, you are preparing for this possibility.

- The release of adrenalin allows the pupils of your **eyes** to dilate in order to let more light and provide keener vision.

- When you are in danger or under stress, extra platelets are released to help clotting of the **blood** and slow bleeding. Just in case the saber-toothed tiger takes a bite out of you.

As well, sugars and fat are released into the blood to give you extra strength and fuel. The hormone cortisol is released to help keep your body on guard for long periods of time. When you experience a "vigilance reaction," the blood thickens with the help of adrenalin and cortisol. This sticky blood can attach itself to any fat build-ups you may have on the inside of your arteries. In time, this will narrow the arteries and may even block them completely, causing a heart attack or stroke.

When adrenalin is released, it affects your whole body. It is not selective. You can't choose to have your heart speed up and your breathing slow down. It's all or nothing.

WHAT STRESS DOES TO YOUR BODY

When it comes to health and disease, the body and mind are closely related. Recent estimates are that 75–80% of all diseases are caused or aggravated by stress.

Stress reduces the effectiveness of the immune system, making you more prone to illness. When you are stressed, a cold or a flu bug that you could normally fight off will take hold and make you sick. You can probably recall a time in your life when you were under stress that caused insomnia (difficulty sleeping), among other problems. It doesn't take long to get run down when you lose sleep, and then you get sick.

Cholesterol. An elevated level of cholesterol in the blood is a major risk factor for heart disease and strokes. Cholesterol sticks to the inside of the blood vessels, clogging them up. The Heart and Stroke Foundation have been telling us this for years. When the stress response takes place, our bodies release cholesterol to meet the energy demands our muscles may make if we have to fight or run. Since it's unlikely we will use up all the cholesterol that is released, we develop an elevated cholesterol level.

High blood pressure is called the silent killer. Many people have high blood pressure and do not realize it. When the pressure in your arteries (blood vessels that carry the blood away from your heart) is increased, the heart has to work harder to pump the blood. This extra strain on the heart is not good. High blood pressure increases the chance of a heart attack or a stroke. Stress is a major contributor to cardiovascular disease, and cardiovascular disease is a major contributor to heart attacks and strokes.

In most cases, blood pressure can be controlled easily, quite often just by changing your diet and/or reducing your salt intake. Sodium retains water in your body, which can increase blood pressure. Other people may need medications called diuretics or water pills, which make you urinate more and reduce the fluid in your body.

Reduced immune system. When cortisol is released in the blood because of the Fight or Flight response, it may kill off some of the white blood cells, which help to fight infection and disease. In other words, the immune system is weakened. You get sick more easily and your illnesses last longer.

Cancer. Some cancer cells are always floating around in the body. Under normal conditions, the immune system can handle this. The white blood cells attack the cancer cells and destroy them. It is believed that reduced effectiveness of the immune system may allow the cancerous cells to spread. There is much still to learn about stress and cancer.

Muscle pain. A common response to stress is to tighten muscles throughout the body. You may not even realize you are doing this, until the resulting backaches and sore neck muscles let you know.

Jaw clenching. Many people clench their jaws without noticing what they are doing. Quite often, the result is pain just below the ear. Left untreated, it can turn into a more serious condition called Temperalmandibular Joint Dysfunction (TMJ).

At one time, I noticed constant pain in my jaw area. When I went to the physician, the first thing he asked me was whether I was under a lot of stress. Of course I said "No." (Sometimes you just don't want to admit it.) But I

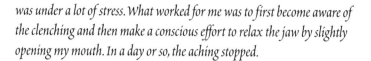

was under a lot of stress. What worked for me was to first become aware of the clenching and then make a conscious effort to relax the jaw by slightly opening my mouth. In a day or so, the aching stopped.

Headaches. Many people suffer tension headaches when they are under stress. Just as you may get a sore back from increased muscle tension, you can get a headache from the tension in and around the jaw, neck, forehead and eyes.

Ulcers are caused by bacteria. When a person is under stress, the body may secrete certain juices that can aid in the formation of ulcers.

Irritable bowel syndrome. There are various signs and symptoms of an irritable bowel: excessive gas, abdominal pain and tenderness, constipation and/or diarrhea.

WHAT STRESS DOES TO YOUR MIND AND EMOTIONS

Loss of appetite and weight loss/Increased appetite and weight gain. When people are worried or going through difficult times, they often lose their appetites. You may recognize this problem, in friends and family or in yourself. The last thing you want to do is to eat. The pounds just melt away, and your clothes get baggier. This is not a good way to lose weight.

At the other extreme, some people react to stress by eating. They find that they are always hungry and constantly eating.

Increased cigarette smoking. Some people light up one cigarette after another to "calm their nerves." The nicotine in cigarettes is a stimulant; it will not calm you down.

Increased alcohol consumption. Added stress can be the breaking point that puts a person into the "problem drinker" category. This can have devastating effects on the family.

Loss of ability to make decisions. People who are under stress have their minds filled with things they have to work out or do, and as a result often cannot concentrate on the task at hand. Stress can affect your ability to reason and make decisions.

Loss of sense of humor. Nothing seems funny when you are under heavy stress. People who can laugh during stressful times usually do better than those who can't. Laughter is a great release.

Paranoia. You think that everyone is out to get you, and that the boss, fellow employees and your spouse are talking about you behind your back. (Maybe they are!)

Decreased sex drive. Nothing more has to be said.

Lack of interest in hobbies or pastimes. Something that you once found exciting and interesting—such as golf, fishing or music—no longer interests you. You find that you have no time for it; you are just too busy.

Anger. Some people vent their stress by losing control and blowing up. A once-calm person may suddenly explode when dealing with a seemingly minor situation. This can be extremely dangerous. A person could do something he or she will deeply regret later. If you feel this could happen to you, seek professional help immediately. (The person you wave your finger at in the traffic jam may be twice your size and really angry about your salute.)

Feeling out of control. You might feel hopeless, as if nothing you do will help you get back in control.

Crying or weeping. Severe stress can cause you to cry for no apparent reason. This is not a good sign. You should get some help.

Social withdrawal. People who are confronted with problems may react by withdrawing from their friends and families, even though it is during troubled times that they most need other people.

The ripple effect. Quitting a job because of stress can lead to financial problems and problems at home. Your home problems will almost certainly spill over into the workplace. Your stress may affect your family, co-workers, friends and almost anyone you come into contact with. Early recognition of stress can help stop this ripple effect before it starts.

Remember, we may be out of control of the situation, but we can control our response to the situation!

A young man who is normally friendly and laid back was about to be married. In a grocery store, the young man came close to starting a fist fight — a reaction that was totally out of character for him. The stress of getting married probably had something to do with it.

Managing Stress: The Fundamentals

Although there is no one quick fix for stress, there are several different ways of managing stress that many people have found useful. We are all individuals. What works for one person might not work for the next. Probably, a combination of these approaches will give the best results.

As with any new skill, methods of managing stress take time to learn. Don't expect miracle cures right away, and take enough time to give these options a chance. They have worked for thousands of other people. They work for me. They can work for you.

"Life is too short. Live it up."—Nikita Khrushchev

ADDRESS THE PROBLEM

Relaxation techniques will help you relax, but they will not make your problem go away. To reduce your stress, you have to get to the root of the problem. This sometimes takes a lot of time, effort and soul-searching. It's worth the trouble required to constructively focus on the problem and concentrate on how to fix it. Different choices will come to light that you never thought of before.

These are steps you need to take:

1. Identify what the real problem is.

2. Address ways to solve it.

3. Put these ideas into action!

Also, never be afraid to seek professional help when your problems seem too big to handle alone.

KNOW THAT YOU HAVE A CHOICE

You cannot always control what happens to you. If you lose your job in a layoff or a loved one dies, these things are beyond your control. The one thing you can control, though, is your response to the situation. Different people will respond to the same situation in very different ways.

One person may lose a child to cancer or an accident and feel extremely bitter towards the world for years—or even for the rest of his life. Another person who is in the same circumstances may—after the initial trauma—volunteer to help raise money for cancer research or work for an organization that helps grant wishes to terminally ill children. This second person focuses his energy on helping make the world a better place, instead of being bitter. Everyone can make this choice.

Viktor E. Frankl, an internationally renowned psychiatrist, spent several years in Nazi death camps under extremely harsh conditions. In his book *Man's Search For Meaning*, Frankl writes:

> *We who lived in concentration camps can remember the men who walked through the huts comforting others, giving away their last piece of bread. They may have been few in number, but they offer sufficient proof that everything can be taken from a man but one thing: the last of human freedoms—to choose one's attitude in any given set of circumstances, to choose one's own way (p. 86).*

Here are some of the choices you have in your life:
- I choose not to worry about the things I cannot control.
- I choose to smile more.
- I choose to spend more time with my kids.
- I choose to eat nutritious foods instead of foods that will harm me.
- I choose to learn more about my job so I am more valuable to my place of work.
- I choose not to let the irritating person at work get to me.
- I choose to look at other career options in case of downsizing; for example, starting my own business.

- I choose to network with people as much as I can (in case of downsizing).
- I choose to live within my means. If I have to, I will seek help from a financial planner.
- I choose to exercise regularly to improve my health.
- I choose to accept change and work with it rather than trying to fight it.
- I choose not to let little things bother me.
- I choose not to blow my horn at the idiot driver in front of me.
- I choose to hang up and not argue with telephone solicitors.
- I choose to get enough sleep each night.
- I choose to tell other people about the things they do that bother me.
- I choose to have a choice.

I choose to choose my own reaction to each situation!

As you begin choosing your own response to situations, you will start to realize that you have more control over yourself than you did before. The usual result of making such choices is a great reduction in stress. When you make your own decisions about how you react to situations, you are in control. When you are in control, there is less stress.

NEW REALITY + PERSONAL REACTION = STRESS LEVEL

More than any time in history, mankind faces a crossroads. Our path leads to despair and utter hopelessness, the other, to total extinction. Let us pray we have the wisdom to choose correctly.
—*Woody Allen*

GET ENOUGH SLEEP

Anyone who has been under stress knows how hard it can be to get a good night's sleep. The mind seems to go crazy thinking about all the problems of the day and the ones to come tomorrow, and the next day and the next. Even if you manage to fall asleep, you might wake up in the middle of the night, time after time.

When you don't sleep properly, the stress increases. Your immune system weakens and you get sick. Getting a good night's sleep is essential for a healthy life.

1. Go to bed at a reasonable time. Many people work long hours and then come home and work some more. Aim for eight hours' sleep each night and try to get to bed at the same time every night.

2. Have a sleep routine. Follow the same routine every night: read a book, have a warm drink, take a bath, watch television or do whatever else helps you to relax. If reading and watching television are a part of your activities while you are awake, they may not be suitable bedtime habits. Find out what works for you. Establish a routine that your body quickly adapts to and expects at bedtime.

3. Avoid stimulants. At bedtime, avoid coffee, pop, tea, chocolate or any other beverages or food that contain caffeine or other stimulants. Also avoid caffeine in the late afternoon and evening.

4. Don't eat before bed. As you digest food, your heart beats faster and your intestines work harder. Indigestion and heartburn can keep you up for hours.

5. Exercise daily. Since exercise tires you out mentally as well as physically, regular exercise can improve the quality of your sleep. Many times when your stress response kicks in, you cannot get rid of the extra energy that is produced.

6. Have a comfortable bed. Children can sleep soundly on any type of surface or in any position, but most adults do not sleep well unless their bed has a good box spring and mattress. A good night's sleep is worth more than money.

7. Keep the room dark. In northern latitudes, the sun shines until 11:00 p.m. in June. Shift workers are often trying to sleep at 10:00 a.m. Blinds and curtains that are heavy enough to block out light, along with blindfolds, are very good investments. Carry the blindfolds with you when you travel, as many hotel rooms seem to have a street light just on the other side of your window. (The same window where the curtains don't quite close!)

one thousand four hundred & ninety one... one thousand four hundred & ninety two... one thousand ....

LEARN TO RELAX

There are many different ways to relax. What works for one person may not work for another. Try the methods described in this section with an open mind and see what suits you best.

Breathing. When you breathe, you suck in oxygen and blow out carbon dioxide. In this way, you provide every cell in your body with a much-needed fresh supply of oxygen.

The diaphragm is a dome-shaped muscle that separates your abdominal cavity (guts) from your chest cavity. When you breathe, the diaphragm moves down and increases the lung space. When this happens, the air pressure in the lungs is lowered. Air rushes into your lungs until the pressure is equal. When you exhale, the opposite happens. The diaphragm moves up, decreasing the lung area. This raises the air pressure in the lungs and forces air out of the body.

People are usually not aware of their breathing. They just breathe. With practice, though, you can make your breathing more efficient. And by becoming conscious of your breathing, you can relax.

Abdominal breathing—system used by singers, actors and public speakers to help them project their voices—promotes relaxation.

1. Lie on your back and make yourself comfortable. Have your feet a comfortable distance apart. Close your eyes.

2. Place one hand on your abdomen and the other on your chest. As you breathe, notice which hand is going up as you breathe.

"There is more to life than increasing its speed."
—*Gandhi*

3. Inhale and exhale very smoothly. Notice the air dropping into your lungs, staying there and flowing out as you exhale.

4. Make a conscious effort to pull in your abdominal muscles in as you exhale. It will be easier if you use your hand to put slight pressure on your abdominal muscles. Or try using two heavy books. When you breathe in, notice your abdominal muscles pushing out.

Note: Abdominal breathing can also be practiced while sitting.

5. Place your hands by your side and continue breathing in this fashion. When you exhale, your abdominal muscles suck in. When you inhale, they bulge out. Be aware of your breathing. Notice the air dropping in and flowing out. This should be effortless.

6. Continue breathing in and out, remaining conscious of your breathing. Do this for four to five minutes until this becomes your natural way of breathing.

Muscle relaxation is a simple technique that people have used for thousands of years. I first read about it in *The Archie Moore Story*, a book about the light-heavyweight boxing champion of the world in the 1950s. Archie Moore was able to use this relaxation technique in a noisy room and feel rejuvenated after 20 minutes.

1. Find a quiet place and lie down. (You can lie on the floor or on a bed.) You might also practice this technique in a comfortable chair. Get very comfortable, and notice your breathing. Breathe from your diaphragm. Let the air drop into your lungs and flow out.

2. Get ready to consciously relax each part of your body, one part at a time. Relaxing means no movement. If you are scratching or twitching, your muscles aren't relaxing.

3. Focus your mind on your right foot, and relax all parts of your foot: your toes, instep and heel. Change your focus to your calf muscle. Feel the relaxation. Work the relaxation up to your knee, then your thigh. Your hip is next. Concentrate on your totally relaxed leg.

4. Now focus on your left foot. Follow the same technique as for the right foot, relaxing your left foot, calf, knee, thigh and hip.

5. Focus on your right hand. Feel your fingers relax, and your palm and wrist. Then relax your forearm, elbow, bicep and shoulder. Focus on your whole arm. It should be totally relaxed.

6. Focus on your left hand. Relax the fingers, palm and wrist. Repeat the sequence for your left arm and shoulder. Both arms and shoulders are now relaxed.

7. Focus on your spine. Relax your back. Concentrate on your lower back and let it relax. Let the relaxation slowly and smoothly flow up your spine. Your whole back is now totally relaxed.

8. Continue relaxing your spine and move up into your neck. Relax all the muscles in your neck.

9. Your chest is next. Let the air drop into your lungs. Relax your chest and abdominal muscles. Notice them relaxing.

10. Relax your abdominal muscles. Feel them relaxing

11. Relax the muscles in your face. Let your jaw drop slightly open. Relax your tongue. Relax all the muscles in your face. Close your eyes. Your whole body is relaxed.

12. Stay in this totally relaxed state for five to ten minutes.

13. When you come out of the relaxation state, open your eyes and stretch slowly. Roll over to one side and stay there for a few seconds. Standing up too quickly could make you dizzy. Stand up, slowly and carefully.

Once you have learned the basics of this technique, you may want to change the sequence to suit you. As with any new skill, you have to practice.

The progressive muscle relaxation technique, developed by Dr. Edmund Jacobson, is very similar to the muscle relaxation technique described above. Progressive muscle relaxation can also be practiced lying down or sitting in a comfortable chair. The difference is that you tense each muscle for five seconds before relaxing it. Tensing the muscle first reminds you what the tension feels like. Then, when you relax the muscle, you feel the tension fade away. You may need some practice before you can tense only one muscle group at a time instead of tensing your whole body.

1. Tense all the muscles in your body, from head to toes. Feel the tension. Hold the tension for about five seconds and then exhale. As you exhale, relax your muscles completely.

2. In the sequence that you prefer—starting at the head or at the feet—tense each of the individual muscle groups (hands, arms, shoulders, legs, spine and so on) for at least five seconds. Then, let them relax.

Tensing the muscles for longer than ten seconds could cause you to develop cramps. Be sure not to miss any parts of your body. Include the forehead, tongue, muscles around the eyes and every muscle group, right down to your toes.

Visualization is similar to day dreaming. Visualization involves travelling in your mind to an enjoyable place, without leaving the room. Everyone does this at least occasionally, and some people do it often.

Your imagination is a powerful tool that you can use to help reduce your stress. Just as your mind can worry you into illness, it can also take you away from a stressful situation.
Try this visualization technique:

1. Lie down in a quiet place. Loosen any tight clothing and close your eyes.

2. Relax any muscles that are tense.

3. Picture yourself in one of your favorite, peaceful places: a park, the porch of your cabin, the top of a mountain, a mossy place by a small creek…Just about any place of your choice will do, but for most people a rock concert would not be a good choice.

4. Create a vivid mental picture of the place. See yourself arriving there.

5. See yourself lying down and getting comfortable.

6. Bring all of your senses into play. Smell the air, see the surroundings, feel the breeze on your face, touch the grass you

are lying on. Listen to the sounds around you. Relax and enjoy yourself.

7. You may want to include some thoughts or affirmations such as, "I am becoming very relaxed."

If you practice visualizing two or three times a day, within a short time this will become a useful tool.

Yoga, an ancient Indian art, has gained popularity in the West. Once learned, it has other benefits besides mental and physical relaxation. It also increases flexibility, muscle strength and endurance.

Massage therapy is gaining popularity in the medical field. Besides helping to heal injured muscles, it is a very beneficial relaxation technique. Anyone who has had a professional massage will agree. If you are feeling pressured, try making an appointment with a registered massage therapist.

EAT A HEALTHY DIET

There are thousands of books that go into great detail about proper nutrition. Here, I will provide only a few basic guidelines.

During the first several years that I worked in Emergency Services, I became an expert on junk food. My diet and eating habits sucked. I am now changing this, and I feel better.

Good nutrition helps fight off stress and reduces the risk of cardiovascular disease. It helps you live longer. Poor nutrition can cause or contribute to heart attacks, strokes, cancer, constipation, obesity, migraine headaches and much more.

A balanced diet should contain:

Carbohydrates	-	50% of total calorie intake
Protein	-	15–20 %
Fats	-	30–35%
Fiber	-	50 grams per day

There are simple and complex **carbohydrates**. Simple carbohydrates are found in foods such as refined white sugar, alcohol and white flour. Most simple carbohydrates do not

My favorite place to visualize is the top of Mt. Wilcox, near the Columbia Icefields. I worked in that area for many years and hiked to the top of the peak on a regular basis. I see myself reaching the top and getting in a comfortable position. I see the cars on the Jasper - Banff highway, far below. I see the expanse of the Icefields and all the mountains around. I feel warm sun and cool breeze at the same time. I hear the breeze, but nothing else.

contain fiber. Consequently, the body absorbs them quickly; they go directly into the blood stream. When you are stressed, you have enough sugar in your blood already. You do not need this extra sugar.

Complex carbohydrates contain a certain amount of fiber, which helps to slow down the digestive process and keep the sugar level in the blood at an appropriate level. At the same time, the body can easily convert complex carbohydrates into energy.

Protein is important for growth, and it helps us fight disease. But since protein is found in most foods, we tend to eat more protein than we need. And when we eat too much protein, it turns into fat.

Most North Americans consume too much **fat**. Many of us have diets that are 45% fats, instead of the 30–35% that is recommended.

Fiber, also called roughage, is good for us, and most of us don't have enough of it in our diets. Fiber, which is the parts of plants that are not digested, acts like a sponge. It absorbs unneeded substances and carries them out though the bowel system. It keeps us regular. It is also very filling, so it prevents us from pigging out on the bad things—simple carbohydrates and excessive fat.

To prevent dehydration, drink at least eight glasses of **water** a day. When you stay "hydrated," you flush out the bad things in your blood stream and keep your skin looking attractive and healthy.

Ask your doctor, a public health unit or your company nurse about the standard recommended diets.

A NOTE ON SHIFT WORK

Approximately 30% of the workforce is involved in shift work. Many industries and services, such as the police force, fire departments and convenience stores operate 24 hours a day.

One of the biggest problems that shift workers face is not getting enough sleep. I have worked shifts for over seventeen years, and I have never slept as well when on evening or night shifts as when working days. Our bodies seem to expect to be active during the day and resting at night. Some useful information about sleeping has already been included in this section. It also helps to be especially aware of your diet and to avoid caffeine.

Shift workers face special challenges regarding diet. Since they don't eat breakfast, lunch or supper at the normal hours, they are not likely to eat with their families and probably have to fend for themselves. The result is often a quick and easy meal that may not be healthy. When you substitute junk food (which normally contains a lot of fat) for regular meals, you will find it harder to fall asleep. Eating at irregular hours can also increase digestive problems.

For many shift workers, ingesting caffeine is part of the routine. Caffeine, a stimulant, not only interferes with sleep but can also cause digestive problems. Caffeine is a diuretic (it makes you urinate), so it may interrupt your sleep by causing you to visit the washroom just after you fall asleep. And, caffeine can elevate your perceived stress level because it increases your alertness, which will already be in high gear if you are stressed.

Chapter

5

Other
Strategies
for
Managing
Stress

You may wish to do further research on the other stress management strategies that are briefly described in this section. Start with the reference list at the back of this book.

SELF TALK

A lot of people talk to themselves, and most people believe what they tell themselves. For example, if you think "I can do anything I try" or "I like myself," you will develop a positive self-image. If you think "I am a failure" or "I can't do that," you will live up to the expectations you have set for yourself.

Try continually repeating lines like these when you're in stressful situations.

1. I can do anything I try.

2. I like myself.

3. I have the willpower to lose 30 pounds.

4. I get nervous sometimes, but so does everyone.

5. This job will be difficult, but I can do it.

Once again, this is a new skill. It will take practice. Don't expect great changes overnight. The idea is to replace your negative thoughts with positive ones. You can choose what you think about. Feeding your mind with positive thoughts will greatly increase your confidence and self-esteem. But it does take time.

If you believe you can, or if you believe you can't, you're right.

—Henry Ford

NOT WORRYING

Almost everyone has something to worry about, and some have more worries than others. Interestingly, though, the amount of worrying that people do is not necessarily related to the worry they really have.

Being able to control your worry is a very special skill. It takes some work. The following ideas for controlling worrying are based on Dale Carnegie's excellent suggestions in *How to Stop Worrying and Start Living*. (I highly recommend this book.)

1. Look at the situation and honestly consider the worst possible outcome. If you will still be alive after the worst-case scenario, you are a lot better off than others. If you won't be thrown into jail for the rest of your life, you are better off than some. In most situations, the worst-case scenario is really not as bad as you might first think.

2. After considering the worst possible outcome, work at accepting the situation. Once you realize it won't be the end of the world, you can relax and proceed to the next step.

3. Focus on improving the current situation. What can you do? What kind of help can you get? You'll be amazed at the ideas that pop into your head when your energy and thoughts are focused.

   "In Newfoundland, we have a lot to worry about, but we just don't bother to worry."

   —Marilyn Hogan, O'Riley's Pub, St. John's, Newfoundland

ACCEPTING CHANGE

The world is changing faster than anyone living 20 years ago could ever have imagined. Few people thought, even ten years ago, that we would be carrying our computers around—computers more powerful than ones that were 50 times that size in the 1970s. And whoever thought that so many full-time jobs would turn into part-time jobs, contract work and self-employment?

"And that's
the way it is."
—Walter Cronkite

Change is going to happen, whether people want it or not. To make things easier on yourself, you must accept change.

Trying to fight change will get you nowhere. Learn to go with the flow and be prepared for the future.

The following list covers just a few of the things you can do to help you deal with job security issues in these crazy times. Use these techniques to make yourself more employable. (You could prepare a similar list for accepting change in other aspects of your life.)

Get computer literate. Computers are used for just about everything. So take some computer courses, if you haven't already done so. If you were an employer, who would you hire? Someone who could use a computer or someone you would have to train? An employer may think you lack initiative if you are totally computer illiterate.

Further your education. Take as many courses as you can to make yourself more marketable. Go to night school or take correspondence courses. It has never been easier to further your education. Take courses in writing and public speaking. Being able to communicate effectively is a very powerful tool. Education is fun. Learn!

Stay current in your field. Reading up on your profession or field will help keep you on top. Read magazines and books, or surf the Internet. Do whatever it takes. The more current and knowledgeable you are, the more valuable you are.

Network. Meet people. It's amazing what opportunities come to light when you meet new people. Expanding your contacts is fun, educational and very useful. Joining volunteer organizations or working on community projects can open many doors. You never know when your friends will be able to help you out, or when you can help them out.

LETTING THINGS GO

Have you ever been really ticked off at someone or about something that happened to you? Maybe someone jilted you at the altar. Maybe some boss fired you years ago, and you're still angry. If you refuse to let such things go, you are carrying extra baggage.

Think about the amount of energy you have wasted reliving these events—energy that could have been expended for useful purposes instead of on plotting revenge. It is wise to let things go instead of telling friends and co-workers about it for the thousandth time. They don't want to hear it. Focus your valuable energy on something that will give you good returns.

"To be wronged or robbed is nothing unless you continue to remember it.
—*Confucius*

COUNTING TO TEN

To handle the little stressors you face each day, stop and close your eyes. Take deep breaths as you count to ten. Concentrate on relaxing. This is a simple but effective technique. The hard part is remembering to do it.

BEING ASSERTIVE

Many people have trouble expressing concerns, feelings or emotions. They fail to assert themselves by saying what they need or want. The result is stress that could easily have been avoided. The alternative is to go home and get angry—at the situation and at ourselves, for failing to communicate our feelings. When you are not assertive, people step all over you. If this goes unchecked, your self-esteem goes down, and your stress level goes up.

This is an example of a problem that is becoming more prevalent in today's society.

In many families these days, you could find yourself looking after one or both of your parents. Some parents even move in with their children, which can add a lot of stress to everyone concerned.

This can be a very sensitive situation. Aging parents need more care and supervision. You could find yourself devoting more time to doing extra laundry or possibly giving up your favorite TV show because your parent wants to watch another show. You might become a chauffeur as you take Mother to the doctor's office, physiotherapy or the drugstore. These seemingly minor things can add up to the point where you are on the verge of boiling over.

At this point, you must become assertive otherwise, you will end up resenting or even hating your parent. You have to take charge of this very sensitive situation or it will eat away at you. It could affect all aspects of your life.

Every situation will be different. You could suggest that your Mother's medications be delivered or that she could take a cab for to appointments. You might have to tell her it is time for her to look for a nursing home because you don't have the time to commit to looking after her. After all, you do have your own family to care for. This will never be easy, but sooner or later it will have to be done.

One of the first steps in asserting yourself is making up your mind to do it. Perhaps we avoid asserting ourselves because we are afraid. We need to realize that, first, we have the right to say what we want, and second, we should not be afraid of saying what we need to say.

If you don't run your life somebody else will.
—John Atkinson

You may think you are protecting others, when in fact you are not. You have the right to say what you want to say.

SETTING AND ACHIEVING GOALS

"You have to know what you want to get."
—Gertrude Stein

Many people spend more time planning a vacation than they do planning their lives. If you plan out your goals and work at reaching them, you will have fewer surprises and therefore less stress.

Try making some plans for the following areas of your life:

Career. Start now if you want to take over your boss's job.

Finances. Start planning how you will gain financial freedom and control of your finances.

Physical fitness. Plan to run that marathon you have always dreamed about.

Education. Send for those correspondence courses to get your high school diploma or start earning a college degree.

Recreation. Learn how to sail a boat and plan your cruise around the world.

One man's goal was to climb 52 mountain peaks in the Canadian Rockies that were over 11,000 feet. He completed his goal. He was 53 years old when he started.

The man who starts out going nowhere generally gets there.
—Dale Carnegie

Plan your goals. If you don't know where you are going, it's hard to get there. Take the time to sit down and think about your goals. This can take quite a while, and your list may change. A new goal may become more important than some of the other goals you originally set. This is your first step towards achieving your goals.

Write them down. Record all of your goals in a binder or notebook so you can remind yourself about what you intend to do. You can even put little notes around the house or office as reminders. Out of sight, out of mind.

Be specific. Don't be vague. Don't say, "I will run a marathon," but "I will run the Honolulu Marathon next year on such-

and-such a date." If you plan to be financially independent by a certain time, write down the date. Also, write down how much money you want to have by them. (Be sure to use a large enough piece of paper so all the zeros will fit.)

Don't set unrealistic goals. For most people, becoming independently wealthy within three years is unrealistic. For a first marathon, running a marathon in three hours may be unrealistic. Don't set yourself up for disappointment.

If you don't reach your goal by the specific time you have set, remember it's not the end of the world. At least you are moving forward. Don't use this as an excuse, though. Strive for your goals.

Break big goals into smaller goals. Setting small goals along the path to your ultimate goal is an amazingly effective and fun way of getting where you want to go. When I wrote my book, *I Won't Be In to Work Today, Preventing Injuries at Home, Work and Play* my goal was to write one chapter every ten days. This seemed much easier than writing a whole book. You will be surprised to see how quickly the small goals add up to make something much bigger.

"A journey of a thousand miles starts with a single step."
—*Ancient Chinese proverb*

Celebrate reaching your goals. When you reach a goal, be happy about it. Celebrate, tell people, go out for dinner. Take a day off. Do something you enjoy. You have worked hard, so enjoy the moment.

"There is no substitute for hard work."
—*Thomas Edison*

"We may allow ourselves a brief period of rejoicing."
—*Sir Winston Churchill, on the day World War II ended*

Be relentless. There is a difference between people who plan goals and people who plan goals and achieve them. People who achieve goals actually do the grunt work.

You have to be consistent. You have to work at things. They will not happen by themselves. It takes hard work.

MANAGING YOUR TIME

"Time is on my side... yes it is."
—*Rolling Stones*

People often complain that they don't have enough time. Everyone has 1,440 minutes in every day and 10,080 minutes in a week. No more, no less.

Busy people have to become aware of how they spend their time.

Turn off the television. Many people spend hours in front of the tube watching shows that provide absolutely no benefit. I'm not saying you should not watch TV, but don't let the television get in the way of your work or your goals. You can free up a lot of time by shutting it off until the work is done. The television can also be a stressor. Watching an hour of bad news or a disturbing show before going to bed can keep anyone awake.

Ask yourself, "Did I use my time effectively today?" If your answer is "No," try to figure out the where and the why. Think about where you spent your time and where you wasted it. Then, on the next day, try to improve the way you use your time.

Use a day planner. Invest in one of the many systems that are available for planning your week, month or year. Take the time to learn how to use your system effectively... And consistently.

Take the time to plan your week. Taking a half an hour once a week to plan—perhaps on a Sunday—will help you stay organized. Write down your goals, commitments, workout times and any other engagements you may have.

Prioritize your list. Beside each task you plan, indicate whether it is Priority "A" (thing that has to be done) or Priority "B" (thing that is important but could possibly wait). You may also have Priority "C" items that would be nice to do, but it's no big deal if you don't.

Do one task at a time. When you start a task, try to stay focused on it until it is done. Working on several things at the same time is not only distracting, but usually a time waster. You will be impressed when you see what you can accomplish by focusing effort on one job at a time.

Stay on top of your work. If you start and work on important tasks immediately instead of procrastinating, they are more likely to be completed on time. Most people don't do that. They wait until the due date is close and the situation is urgent. The result is an increased stress level.

Delegate tasks. If you hate cutting the lawn and can hire the neighbor's kid to cut it for six bucks, you have just saved yourself some time. Hiring a maid can free up a lot of time. Look for work that you can pass along to someone else.

Learn to say no. Many people accept responsibilities even though they don't really want to take them on. For example, you would love to coach your child's baseball team, and someone has asked you to do it. You have so many things on the go just now that you know you won't have time for coaching, but you say you will anyway. You have just created a lot more stress for yourself. Never be afraid to say no.

Take a speed reading course. If you have to do a lot of reading to stay current in your profession, or if you just enjoy reading, I strongly recommend taking a speed reading course. These courses are available at colleges, or through home study with audio tapes and a workbook. After the course, you might not be able to scan pages at amazing speed, but you will save countless hours throughout the years.

Don't finish reading every book you start. It's a waste of time to finish a book you feel is terrible. If you are not receiving any benefit, pick up another book instead. Follow the same rule when watching television shows. Do you sit through a 90-minute movie and then complain that it is the worst movie you have ever seen?

LAUGHING AT YOURSELF

It is a great gift to be able to laugh at yourself and the situations you find yourself in. Laughter can add years to your life. When things get tough, try to look at the lighter side. Granted, this will probably not work when there is a death in the family. But in many situations a laugh will make you feel a whole lot better.

Viktor Frankl (*Man's Search for Meaning*) describes how humor can allow a person to rise above any situation, even if it's just for a few seconds. And let's remember, he was talking about Nazi concentration camps, where there was nothing to laugh about.

GETTING AND STAYING ORGANIZED

For many years I cursed myself and lost money because of my messy office and poor filing system. I now have a system for keeping things organized. And I use it. The result? I don't have to do things twice because I lost the first letter, report or book.

Have you ever needed some information that you couldn't find, even though you knew you had it in the house or in your office? Knowing where you keep important papers, insurance policies, car keys, tickets for the concert, old invoices, warranties and countless other important documents not only reduces stress but also saves time and money. Get a filing system that will suit your needs... And use it on a consistent basis.

LOOKING IN THE MIRROR

Did you ever work with someone who was hard to get along with? Someone who didn't know or care about his job and who pushed extra work on to you? Someone who had a bad attitude and thought everyone else at work was a jerk? Perhaps the person had financial problems and always whined about them—while driving an expensive new car.

Everyone can relate to these descriptions. You may even have one of these types of people in your own family. Or in your own skin?

It is difficult to admit that you (heaven forbid) may have a fault. It is even more difficult to admit that you may be causing a lot of your own problems. If things aren't going the way you would like, try looking in the mirror and asking yourself these questions:

1. Am I having problems at work because I don't know my job as well as I should?

2. Am I refusing to accept change?

3. Are my financial problems caused by living beyond my means?

4. Is alcohol causing many of my personal problems?

5. Am I really stubborn?

6. Is my family right when they say I'm a nasty SOB and I'm hard to live with?

These are just a few of the hundreds of questions you can ask yourself. I'm sure you can think of more. Ask the questions that pertain to your stress, and give honest answers. Find out if you are the cause of some of your stress.

Close friends are good to have, not just because they will help you on moving day, but because they will listen to you when you are having problems or are under a lot of stress. It can really help to have someone to talk to.

Professional counsellors owe much of their success to their ability to listen attentively. The people you meet in a bar are probably not interested in your problems. In fact, that is most likely the last thing they want to hear about.

"One experimental group of rabbits that were fed high-cholesterol diets did not develop hardening of the arteries at nearly the rate of a similar control group. The difference was support: the rabbits who had the lower rate of disease were petted, talked to and given regular individual attention."
—Dr. Robert S. Eliot and Dennis L. Breo, "Is It Worth Dying For?"

Some people try to deal with their problems by them-selves—perhaps because they don't have a support system or because they feel that only weak people need help in handling problems and stress. This is one of the worst situations you can put yourself into. Never be afraid to seek help from those who are close to you and from professionals.

Many companies have confidential Employee Assistance Programs that are designed to help with substance abuse, depression, stress and other problems. These companies realize that keeping their employees healthy and happy is a good investment. If you don't have access to a program like this, look for counsellors or psychologists in the Yellow Pages. In rural areas, call the nearest hospital or health unit to find out what professional help is available in your community.

It takes a strong person to seek help.

Epilogue

In my work as a paramedic, I have witnessed extreme cases of stress-related problems, including approximately 700 heart attacks that often involved people who were close to my own age (43 at the time of writing).

I have learned that such problems can be prevented, or at least reduced. You can choose to manage your stress. It is your decision. And, remember, that if you let stress control your life, it could kill you.

The stress management techniques I describe in these pages really work. But, as with learning any new skill, you must give them a chance.

—Martin Lesperance

References

Coren, Stanley. *Sleep Thieves.* New York: Simon & Schuster, 1997.

Carnegie, Dale. *How to Stop Worrying and Start Living—Time-tested methods for conquering worry.* Pocket Books, a division of Simon & Schuster Inc., 1985.

Charlesworth, Edward A. and Ronald G. Nathan. *Stress Management: A comprehensive guide to wellness.* Ballantine Books, 1982.

Eliot, Dr. Robert S. and Dennis L. Breo. *Is It Worth Dying For? How to make stress work for you—not against you.* Bantam Books, 1989.

Frankl, Victor. *Man's Search for Meaning.* New York: Washington Square Press.

Hanson, Peter G., M.D. *The Joy of Stress: How to make stress work for you.* Second edition. Hanson Stress Management Organization, 1986.

Jones, Dr. Hillary. *I'm Too Busy to Be Stressed: How to recognize and relieve the symptoms of stress.* Hodder & Stoughton, 1997.

McWilliams, Peter, *Life 101.* Prelude Press, 1994

National Safety Council. *Stress Management.* Boston: Jones and Bartlett, 1995.

Patel, Dr. Chandra. *The Complete Guide to Stress Management.* New York: Plenum Press, 1991.

Silber Lee. *Time Management for the Creative Person.* Three Rivers Press, 1998

Williams, Redford, M.D., and Virginia Williams, Ph.D. *Anger Kills: Seventeen strategies for controlling the hostility that can harm your health.* New York: Harper Perennial, 1993.

THE LIFE EVENT TEST

The following self-test allows you to rate your own life events to help determine your personal level of stress.

Simply check off the items that apply to you. On completion, add up the point values of all the items checked. If your score is 300 or more, statistically you stand an almost 80 percent chance of getting sick in the near future. If your score is 150 to 299, the chances are about 50 percent. At less than 150, about 30 percent.

LIFE EVENT		POINTS
_____	Death of spouse	100
_____	Divorce	73
_____	Marital separation	65
_____	Jail term	63
_____	Death of close family member	63
_____	Personal injury or illness	53
_____	Marriage	50
_____	Fired from work	47
_____	Marital reconciliation	45
_____	Retirement	45
_____	Change in health of family member	44
_____	Pregnancy	40
_____	Sex difficulties	39
_____	Gain of new family member	39
_____	Business readjustment	39

_____	Change in financial state	38
_____	Death of a close friend	37
_____	Change to different line of work	36
_____	Change in number of marital arguments	35
_____	Mortgage or loan for major purchase	31
_____	Foreclosure of mortgage or loan	30
_____	Change in responsibilities at work	29
_____	Son or daughter leaving home	29
_____	Trouble with in-laws	29
_____	Outstanding personal achievement	28
_____	Spouse begins or stops work	26
_____	Begin or end school	26
_____	Change in living conditions	25
_____	Revision of personal habits	24
_____	Trouble with boss	23
_____	Change in work hours or conditions	20
_____	Change in residence	20
_____	Change in schools	20
_____	Change in recreational habits	19
_____	Change in church activities	19
_____	Change in social activities	18
_____	Mortgage or loan for lesser purchase	17
_____	Change in sleeping habits	16
_____	Change in number of family get-togethers	15
_____	Change in eating habits	15
_____	Vacation	13
_____	Christmas	12
_____	Minor violations of the law	11

Reprinted with permission from the **Journal of Psychosomatic Research.** Vol. 11, Thomas H. Holmes and Richard H. Rahe, "The Social Readjustment Rating Scale," pp. 213 to 218, 1967. Elsevier Science Inc., 655 Ave. of the Americas, New York NY 10010-5107

HEART ATTACK (MYOCARDIAL INFARCTION)

A 41-year-old firefighter/emergency medical technician who was extremely fit, ran marathons, stuck to a healthy diet and worked out on a regular basis. There was no family history of heart problems. While working out in the gym one day, he collapsed and died of a heart attack. His co-workers were shocked. Many later recalled that he had often complained of chest pains.

This is a classic story. My experience as a paramedic has taught me that most people who are having a heart attack do not seek medical aid immediately. The man in the above story should have known better. He had responded to many calls involving heart attacks and knew how serious an episode of chest pain can be. He paid for his mistake with his life.

Early recognition of medical problems can determine whether you will leave the hospital in your own car or in a hearse. If you are brought into the hospital shortly after your heart attack has started, your chances are quite good. There are drugs that help. Unfortunately, most people do not take the warning signs of a heart attack or stroke seriously and wait several hours before seeking medical aid.

Like any other muscle, the heart needs a constant supply of oxygen. The heart and all other parts of the body receive oxygen through the blood. When the inside of the arteries in the heart (the vessels that carry the blood away from the heart) plug up because of cardiovascular disease, they can stop the blood flow. When this happens, part of the heart will not receive oxygen and the cells in the heart will die. In other words, the person has a heart attack.

Normally, there are some signs and symptoms, such as these:

- pain or a heavy feeling or squeezing in the chest that may radiate to the jaw, neck or arms
- weakness
- nausea and vomiting (a sick stomach)
- shortness of breath and/or difficulty in breathing
- a feeling of impending doom
- anxiety

If someone experiences any of these signs and symptoms, access Emergency Medical Services immediately.

The pain that occurs during a serious heart attack, which may not be severe, can start without any physical exertion. A heart attack could also feel like a case of indigestion, and it may be very hard to tell the difference. It is very common for a person to deny that anything is wrong.

STROKE (BRAIN ATTACK)

A stroke occurs when the blood flow to the brain is interrupted long enough to cause damage. The blood flow interruption may be caused by a clot that blocks the artery, or the artery may just close up. In some cases the artery ruptures. The blood puts pressure on the brain. A stroke can cause permanent brain damage or result in death.

The signs and symptoms of a stroke include:
- a sudden, severe headache
- unconsciousness
- drooping on one side of the face
- difficulty in speaking
- loss of bladder and bowel control
- paralysis or weakness, usually on one side
- change in the level of consciousness (sleepiness)
- confusion
- unequal pupil size and failure to react to light
- visual disturbances (blindness)

TIA (TRANSIENT ISCHEMIC ATTACK)

A transient ischemic attack (little stroke) has the same signs and symptoms as a stroke, but the signs don't last long—ranging from a few minutes to a few hours. Eventually, the person who has suffered a TIA regains full use of the affected parts. This is a warning that a stroke may happen. Anyone who has a TIA must seek medical help. Many persons have had these warnings and ignored them, and a stroke has followed.

OTHER BOOKS BY MARTIN LESPERANCE:

Kids For Keeps: Preventing Injuries to Children
A MUST for all child care givers!
"If you are a parent, grandparent, educator, coach, baby sitter or child care provider; this book is for you. Whether your motivation is responsibility, love or both, Kids for Keeps will inform and empowers you to make a difference."
—Donna Hastings, Vice-Chair, Basic Trauma Life Support International, Emergency Cardiac Care Coordinator, Heart and Stroke Foundation.

I Won't be in to Work Today: Preventing Injuries at Home, Work and Play
Using actual case histories of injuries he has attended, Martin drives home the point that injuries affect not only the injured persons, but also family, friends and co-workers. This book is an excellent guide to preventing injuries on or off the job.
"A very important concern often neglected by companies is off the job safety. this book is long overdue."
—Merril J. Humphrey, Senior Safety Specialist, Husky Oil Ltd.

Price per book $16.95 plus GST • Volume discounts available.
Single copy price: $23.00 (includes GST and shipping)

HOW TO ORDER:

By Mail:
Send cheque or money order to
Safety Health Publishing Inc.
Unit 432-15403 Deer Run Dr. S.E.,
Calgary AB T2J 6B8

By Fax:
1-403-225-3215
By Telephone:
1-403-225-2011 or 1-888-278-8964
By E-mail:
martin@safete.com

- -

ORDER FORM

☐ Please send me ___ copies of *Kids For Keeps: Preventing Injuries to Children*
☐ Please send me ___ copies of *I Won't be in to Work Today: Preventing Injuries at Home, Work and Play*

Company Name

Name

Address

City   Province   Postal Code

Telephone   Fax   E-mail

Payment by: ☐ Cheque ☐ Credit Card (VISA only)

Card Number

Expiry Date   Signature

SPEECHES AND SEMINARS

Available to speak across North America on the topic of injury prevention, Martin's seminars will help your organization reduce benefit costs by helping employees realize that company benefits are an expensive privilege. Some of his most requested talks include:

I Won't be in to Work Today! Preventing Injuries at Home, Work and Play

Employees will learn:
- company benefits are an expensive privilege
- more injuries happen at home than at the workplace
- the ripple effect of injuries
- that safety should be a 24 hour concern, not to be left at the workplace
- 12 safety tips to keep you safe and healthy

What Do You Mean I'm Stressed? Recognizing and Managing Your Stress

Stress is a serious concern for all employers. More and more employees are taking stress-related leaves. Physicians say that up to 75% of patient visits may be brought on, or worsened by stress. In this presentation, Martin points out that stress is with us and will not go away, but it is how you respond to stress that is the important.

Your employees will learn:
- what stress does to your body
- how dangerous uncontrolled stress is
- how to recognize stress in the early stages
- what to do if you find yourself in a stressful situation
- how to control your stress in your job, family and relationships

Stress is a leading cause of heart disease. In his work as a paramedic, Martin has attended people who have suffered severe heart attacks that have resulted in cardiac arrest; often a consequence of uncontrolled stress. In this dynamic seminar you will learn that you can manage your stress before it manages you.

For more information contact:
Martin Lesperance
1-403-225-2011 or 1-888-278-8964
Or visit Martin at his website: www.safete.com.

Member of the National Speakers Association